# A Moment in Time

Dear Casey,

You are one of the finest human beings I have ever known. Your advice & patience on this project were invaluable. Thank you from the bottom of my heart.

Fondly,
Cathy

# A Moment in Time

*Poems by* **Pearl Simmons**

*Illustrations by Cathy Schuster*

**Children's Hospital of Pittsburgh Foundation**

PITTSBURGH, PENNSYLVANIA

2003

Library of Congress catalog card number: 2003107503
ISBN  0-9742557-0-X

Address correspondence, orders, and other queries to:

**Children's Hospital of Pittsburgh Foundation**
3705 Fifth Avenue
Pittsburgh, PA 15213-2583
www.chp.edu

*Book design by Jennifer Zieserl / Studioluxe*
*jen.studioluxe@verizon.net*

# INTRODUCTION

*Passion, perfection and persistence.*
*Mother and wife, educator and writer, volunteer and organizer.*

These words partially describe Pearl Simmons, but it is difficult to express what she actually meant to her family, friends and the community. Pearl touched the lives of many people because she was involved in a great variety of activities. Since words were an important part of Pearl's life, a group of her friends decided it would be appropriate to collect and illustrate some of the poetry she wrote.

Pearl's life was cut short at the age of 42 in the prime of mothering her three children, teaching parenting classes, writing newspaper columns, and maintaining a busy schedule full of meetings and other commitments.

Within her circle of friends, Pearl was the first person to call and offer genuine help and support after learning of a crisis. She loved people and often was the planner of social gatherings or celebrations. Pearl was a master communicator; she could carry on a conversation with anyone about anything.

She was relied upon as a resource since she maintained files on everything, ranging from household projects to menus of dinner parties to names of doctors. Her impressive organizational skills enabled her to accomplish a great deal more in her 42 years than most people do in a lifetime.

She approached tasks very seriously and often said she felt the need to over-prepare. Pearl set high standards for herself and expected a lot from others as well. Pearl also had a fun side and enjoyed letting her (short) hair down! She had a lightness about her that was defined by her smile and frequent laugh. She had a generous heart and freely gave her time to whomever was in need of it. She could accept others for who they were, even if they were quite different.

Above all, Pearl enjoyed spending time with her family and taking care of them. She truly loved being a mother, wife and daughter. The poetry and prose in this volume show the priority that Pearl placed on family.

If you were lucky enough to know Pearl, these poems will have special meaning. If you did not know her, the images, conviction and clarity of her words will likely leave a lasting impression of her wisdom and gift of expression.

— *Lainey Becker, 2003*

*Pearl Simmons, August 1998*

# ARTIST'S NOTE

Pearl and I were friends for 15 years. We met shortly after she and her husband, Reid, moved to Pittsburgh. Pearl was as devoted a friend as she was a mother. Her death in the summer of 2002 was a terrible shock to her family, friends, and the community. Fortunately, she left a beautiful collection of poetry on motherhood and family. The idea of publishing this book came from the Women's Study Group of Beth El Congregation. In an otherwise helpless situation, it has given me and those who loved Pearl some measure of comfort and an opportunity to work through our loss and grief.

I am honored to have been given the privilege of illustrating Pearl's poetry. I hope that, by having known the Simmons family, I have conveyed a personal touch. I would like to express my deep gratitude to my husband, James, for his never-ending support, to my friends for their wise counsel and assistance, and to my sister, Mary Lou Schmidt, for believing that dreams can come true.

From the bottom of my heart I thank all of the donors, the Children's Hospital of Pittsburgh Foundation — especially Pat Siger and Carol Ashby — and my dear friend Reid Simmons, for this opportunity.

— *Cathy Schuster, April 28, 2003*

*Dedicated with love*
*to*
*Reid, Noah, Rachel, & Joshua*

# CONTENTS

Introduction

Artist's Note

*A Moment in Time* / 13

*My Child, My Soul* / 15

*The Coffee House* / 17

*"But What Do You Do All Day?"* / 19

*Letting Go* / 22

*Morning Glories* / 25

*My Shadow* / 26

*Suburban Mother* / 28

*The Terrorizing Toddler* / 31

*On Borrowed Time* / 34

*My Little Girl* / 36

*What's a Mother For?!* / 38

*Breakfast at Grandma's* / 41

*September Sounds* / 44

*The Last Child* / 46

*The Piano* / 49

*We Were Once a Couple... Now a Family* / 51

*A Mom is Something Other* by Noah Simmons

Epilogue

Donor's Page

# A Moment in Time

Motherhood is a moment in time.
A brief instant, when little else matters.
Your children become the center of your universe.
You lead them where you want them to go;
they follow, and soon take over the lead.

Motherhood is a moment in time when you are the essence of their world.
You are their creator and their teacher.
They look to you for guidance, love, and support.
You look to them for fulfillment.

Motherhood brings new meaning to the word "life."
The birth of a child brings new promises and dreams.
Joy and sorrow become deeper emotions,
linked forever to a child's steps and falls.

A child cries — mother responds.
A child's pain is a mother's pain.
She experiences the depth of her child's emotions
as if they were her own.

The two are separate, yet the same.
One being formed from another, and shaped by her.
Over time they grow apart.
The child spreads new roots,
wandering and searching for its own path.

Motherhood is a fleeting instant when professions don't matter.
The benefits are boundless — a living legacy.
Bonds formed in infancy continue in our children's memories;
their values, dreams, and expectations
forever linked to their earliest beginnings.

We have so much to give our children.
So many ways to share our unending love and devotion.
Time moves on, yet the ties of our souls
are unbroken by its passing.

Our children's emotional well-being must be our priority.
To give them a sense of self-worth and
the strength to deal with life's challenges.
Their future depends on us; they are so sensitive and vulnerable.

We have only a moment in time to teach them,
to guide them, to strengthen them.
A moment passes, and we are left alone.
Yet we live on — through them.

They are our moment in time.

○

# My Child, My Soul

I see my soul reflected in your gaze.
I hear my words in your every phrase.
My movements are in your walk,
your glance, the way you talk.
You are a joy to behold,
My child, my soul.

You are my being, you are my son.
You have such spirit, my lovely one.
Your imagination runs so wide.
Your joy of life is a source of pride,
My child, my soul.

You make my life full,
my journey complete.
You are among my greatest feats.
You fill me with gladness
and ease my sadness.
You are ever-loving
My child, my soul.

These are days to be cherished,
and times to remember.
Today we are bound together.
Tomorrow's changes will come soon, I know,
and a time for us to finally let go,
My child, my soul.

Your precious life has been given to me.
I watch over you endlessly,
afraid to let go, afraid to do wrong.
But I know that you are strong,
My child, my soul.

When we are together
our life is so sweet.
But when you are gone
it seems incomplete,
My child, my soul.

Take my hand and comfort me.
Our love for each other will always be,
a source of strength, a tie that binds.
I am yours and you are mine,
My child, my soul.

○

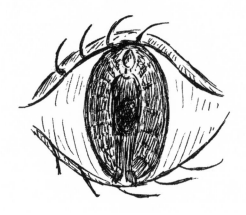

# The Coffee House

A cozy, dimly-lit coffee house.
Spoons tinkling against warm cups.
Soft murmur of people talking,
quiet, passionate, buzzing words.

I sit alone —
blissfully alone!
How did this happen?
I got out early from my appointment.
The coffee house summoned my senses —
inviting me to falter from my expected path.

The urge to follow that path was irresistible.
Reminiscent of days gone by when I could follow a moment's
impulse.
It was a time before nap schedules and carpools.
I was a coffee house fanatic,
and this morning I dared venture back.

What a decadent morning!
Cool, grey and rainy outside.
Inside it is warm, glowing, and exhilarating.
Am I desperate? No,
just a suburban mother with a little free time to be decadent —
for just a little while.

As I sip the last remnants of my cappuccino,
I ponder my next move.
Drive home to three demanding children,
ready to change them, feed them, cater to their every need?
No, I'll hold off just a little longer.

I'll meander over to a boutique
to bask in the glories of high fashion —
free of crumbs, stains, wrinkles, and kid's dribbles.

Oh glorious morning!

○

18

# "But What Do You Do All Day?"

Sometimes I'm asked by people I meet
At parties, in meetings, or out on the street,
"So you gave up your job. You're home without pay.
But what do you do with yourself all day?"

"Aren't kids tiring? Why don't you work?
How do you keep from going berserk?"
I laugh to myself. Bored at home with my brood?
The thought puts me in a jovial mood.

I think of each day, how it starts and it ends,
And somehow on that my answer depends.
From the moment I wake I am on the move,
Helping my kids make their lives run smooth.

At 7:15 the alarm bell rings,
As the birds outside my window sing.
Every morning begins this way,
Signaling the start of a busy day.

I wake up the children and get them dressed,
Feed them breakfast, then clean up the mess.
Put on their shoes and brush their hair.
"Hurry outside, your bus is there!"

I grab some coffee on the way to the shower.
Got to be at nursery school in half an hour!
It's 20 minutes there, then 20 minutes back,
Plus a stop to get money out of the MAC.

Next stop is the market to do some shopping,
Then rush back home, no time for stopping.
I quickly put the groceries away,
Answer phone calls and make lunch for the day.

The school bus drops kindergartners off at eleven.
It feels like it was just a quarter past seven!
Ten minutes later we're back in the car,
For nursery school pick up. It seems so far.

Then off to the doctor to check the kids' ears.
We seem to go fifty times each year!
We try not to waste our precious time,
So while we wait we read books and make rhymes.

We play with toys and talk to each other.
That's "quality time" for children and mother!
The kids unwind, I turn up my gears.
I've lots to do 'til the next school bus appears.

I start making dinner, then vacuum the floor.
Get rid of the crumbs, then find some more.
I throw in some laundry and fold more clothes.
It's amazing how fast the hour goes.

The bathrooms need cleaning. The kids start to fight.
I try to be patient, though no rest is in sight.
After school there's karate; that's another car ride.
Then we head home to play or ride bikes outside.

For me there are always more phone calls to make,
More laundry to fold, food to cook and to bake.
After all I want my kids to be fed,
Happy, well-rounded, and of course well-read!

When bathtime comes our exhaustion is near.
The end of the day is always so dear.
For people who ask if I'm bored staying home,
Whether I get restless or feel the urge to roam.

I answer with a sure and resounding, "No way!"
I really would have it no other way.
My kids are growing and changing each day.
They have so many interesting things to say.

I wouldn't miss this time of their life,
Though being at home can be full of strife.
It tries your patience and tests your skill.
You have to be calm and of very strong will.

But the rewards are many and the drawbacks few.
Each day promises something new.
As your kids discover the world all around,
From colorful flowers to treasures they've found.

And I know that by the end of the day,
I'll have some moments to spend my own way.
The evening is short, but it's oh so sweet.
Just one more load of laundry, then I'll put up my feet!

O

# Letting Go

I can't protect you any more.
I can't make your hurt go away.
I can tell you I love you and show you I care.
I try to help you out when things don't seem fair.

But my power as a mother only goes so far.
I can't always reach the places you are.
I want to be close like we were before.
But you want to move on — to discover what's more.

When you were a baby, I'd hold you tight,
And keep you forever within my sight.
I could satisfy your every need,
It was an easy time for us indeed.

And when you were a toddler and scraped your knee,
You'd hold out your arms and run to me.
I'd kiss where it hurt and make it feel fine.
A hug and kiss worked every time.

I was always the one you turned to then.
I wish it could be like that again.
But now when you're sad you turn away,
And I don't know the words to say.

You're my little boy, but you're growing up fast.
I feel you slipping from my grasp.
I want to hold on, but I know it's time
For me to let go of this child of mine.

I long to protect you, to shield you from pain.
But I have to remind myself time and again,
That you have to experience life on your own,
While I stand back and leave you alone.

You're still so young, but you've already found
How kids can tease when I'm not around.
School kids tease you and call you names.
They make fun of you and play cruel games.

I tell you not to worry, that it'll be alright.
I tell you to be brave, but I can't make things right.
I try to listen and to hold you near,
To give you solace and allay your fear.

I try to be there when the going gets tough.
Sometimes growing up can be so rough.
But I also feel proud of the person you are.
I know that you're strong and that you'll go far.

I realize it's time to start letting go.
I've taught you so much of the things that I know.
As you step forward, I'll take two steps back.
It's not easy for me, but I'll get the knack.

I'm letting go, but I'll never be far.
You can always reach me, wherever you are.
I watch you proudly as you start on your way.
My love goes with you as we start a new day.

O

24

# Morning Glories

It's a September morning, misty and grey.
The kids are off to school today!
I'm so excited, I can hardly wait.
A day of freedom, oh how great!

There's so much that I want to do —
go to the mall, buy something new.
What a rare and glorious treat.
I can even go out to eat!

I'll do some gardening, go for a walk,
Too bad it ends at 3 o'clock!
The life of a mom always depends
on when school starts and the hour it ends.

Summer was fun, playing with kids is grand.
But now that it's over, I can take my own stand!
I'll have coffee at leisure, look over the news,
talk on the phone, and have time to muse.

When the kids aren't about,
I won't miss their shouts,
their crying, their whining,
their constant pining.

It's a September morning,
and I'm alone at last.
I'll treasure the moments —
hope they don't go too fast!

○

# My Shadow

I have a little shadow
That goes everywhere I go.
He follows me throughout the day
As I wander to and fro.

This shadow is quite small.
He has little hands and feet.
And when he toddles after me,
He's really very sweet.

When I wake up in the morning,
Ready to start my day,
I hear my shadow call to me,
Beckoning me to play.

My shadow is always moving.
He can't seem to stand still.
He never lets me stop and rest.
He moves me with his will.

He likes to climb up stairs.
He loves to jump and run.
He follows me outside.
Where he enjoys the sun.

My shadow is a part of me.
We're never far apart.
And when he smiles up at me
His glow warms my heart.

My shadow's getting bigger now.
One day he'll be quite tall.
And then he'll overshadow me,
He'll no longer seem so small.

He'll follow in my footsteps,
Then make a path all his own.
I'll miss my precious shadow.
I'll miss him when he's grown.

O

## Suburban Mother

I have become the suburban mother
I swore I'd never be!
Carpooling back and forth each day
to school, ballet, and karate.

It's a never-ending cycle
that starts and ends each day.
Who is this woman behind the wheel?
"Not me!" I defiantly say.

And yet these are my kids —
it's true.
This is my life;
it's what I do.

Whatever happened to my naïve vows
that I'd never schlep kids like I do right now?
"I'll be different," I used to say.
"I won't stay in my car all day.
I won't let children tie me down.
I'll remain a woman of the town."

But now I have three kids in tow.
I cannot stay home and just lie low.
There are schedules to keep, classes to attend,
friends to meet, and activities on end.

There are soccer games and birthday parties,
museum trips and football rallies,
playgroups, library storytime,
and playgrounds where our kids can climb.

One day recently I'd had enough.
This schedule had become too rough.
I could no longer keep up this pace.
My life had become an unending race.

"Let's stay home!" I bravely shouted.
My kids were shocked and silently pouted.
But slowly they began to take out toys,
to look at books, and make some noise.

They laughed, they joked, they talked to each other.
They had a lot of fun, just sister and brother.
They listened to music, played with dolls,
built some Legos, and played basketball.

And through it all I sat with a book,
then headed to the kitchen for some dinner to cook.
I had finally found the time to be free,
when I could just rest and focus on *me!*

That evening as I kissed my kids good night,
I knew everything would be alright.
I had learned an important lesson that day:
Sometimes you've just got to keep kids home to play!

You don't always have to take them out.
They'll do things at home worth talking about.
And they'll learn to appreciate having each other.
While you become a relaxed and carefree mother!

O

## The Terrorizing Toddler

You are like a tornado
twisting through our home,
causing mass destruction
everywhere you roam.

Wherever you wander
you leave a cluttered path,
with books strewn across the floor
and toys scattered in the bath.

There's markers on the walls,
and crayons on the floor,
ketchup on the ceiling,
and fingerprints on the door.

My friends all say it's just a stage,
they say that it will pass.
But right now you're a terror,
and I'm afraid to cross your path!

You love to play in the bathroom
where you take great delight
in flushing things down the toilet
until they're out of sight.

One day you flushed a toothbrush
'til it went down all the way.
We couldn't figure out why the toilet
didn't work right all that day!

And when you get your hands on
that toothpaste you adore,
you suck it down your little mouth,
then ask for, "More, more, more!"

There's nothing that your hands don't touch,
no place that's safe from your grasp.
You pull down pictures, and open drawers,
emptying their contents fast.

You throw food from your highchair,
and toss juice cups full of juice.
You squish butter into your hair,
as if it were fancy mousse.

Your most expensive habit
is playing with VCR's.
You carefully take out the videotapes
and replace them with Mom's credit cards.

You make sure they're in tight
to ensure a proper fit.
So that when it's taken to be repaired,
they say, "It can't be fixed."

No matter how often we say "Don't touch,"
"Leave it alone," and "Stay out of there,"
you persist in defying our every word,
showing us you just don't care.

You're our terrorizing toddler,
on that we can depend.
We hope that by this time next year,
your antics will come to an end.

Watching over a toddler
puts parents to the test.
It often brings out the worst in us,
though we try to do our best.

If we can just survive these years
with our home and minds intact,
we'll fondly recall these toddler years
and wish we could bring them back!

O

## On Borrowed Time

The day we took our son's crib apart,
I felt a little tug at my heart.
This bed is made of more than just wood.
It's part of my child's babyhood.

I will always remember my son peering through
The bars of his crib to play "peek a boo."
Now he's in a big bed, with pillow and all,
Where he sleeps secured up against the wall.

When I look at him sleeping soundly there,
I see a boy, so big and so fair.
I'm reminded how fast our children grow.
We can't stop time or make it go slow.

We are living together on borrowed time,
Though our fates will forever be intertwined.
We have to savor our moments together,
For we know they will not last forever.

Moving my son from a crib to a bed
Is a rite of passage I anticipated.
It's something every parent goes through,
Get rid of the old and bring in the new.

But lately I've tried to cling to the past,
Knowing this child would be my last.
I record in my memory his every embrace,
And the precious expressions upon his face.

As parents we prepare kids to be on their own,
So they can succeed when they are grown.
We teach them through the books we read,
The values we share, and the lives we lead.

But we ourselves are not always prepared
To give up these special times we've shared.
These milestones mean we're moving on, too.
And must confront a lifestyle that's new.

I ponder this though as I gaze at my son,
And marvel at the person he has become.
I rejoice in the child that he is today,
And try to keep tomorrow a little at bay.

I know we're living on borrowed time,
But right now my child is here and all mine.
As I wait for my son to rise from his bed,
I'll cling to the day that lies just ahead.

O

# My Little Girl

I was so delighted the day you were born.
I had a little girl that I could adorn.
A daughter so pretty, dainty and sweet,
I savor your existence like a delicate treat.

There's more to girls than frills and curls,
lacy pink clothes, and dresses that swirl.
It's true that I like to dress you up fine.
A golden-haired beauty, you are divine.
And I love to buy you patent leather shoes,
bracelets and earrings, and fluffy tutus.

But your beauty transcends the clothes that you wear,
and the cute little bows that you place in your hair.
You're a very special person inside.
You are a joy and source of pride.
You are inquisitive, thoughtful, and curious about life.
Your sense of detail is sharp as a knife.

You have a vivid imagination
that you use in many ways,
animating your little dolls,
creating new worlds as you play.

You are also a determined child.
You know how to make yourself heard.
You do not give up when you have a demand.
You persist 'til you've had the last word.

You are our middle child,
sandwiched in-between two boys
who often get lots of attention,
and who know how to make lots of noise.

Often you just want time alone,
playing with Mommy or Daddy at home.
Wanting to be babied and snuggled by us
and being the focus of our attention and fuss.

We understand that you have to compete,
with your brothers and others — it's no simple feat.
But the bond that we share as parent and daughter
is unique and can be claimed by no other.

Being in the middle can often be tough.
Vying for attention is certainly rough.
But we appreciate how unique you are,
you are our little girl, and you shine like a star.

O

# What's a Mother For?!

I worry that my kids won't make it to school.
I worry they'll be kidnapped by some terrorizing fool.
I worry that they'll trip and fall down stairs.
I worry about their fears and awful nightmares.
What's a mother for?

I worry that their school bus will swerve and crash.
I worry that they'll be covered in a horrible rash.
I worry when they sleep, I worry when they eat,
I worry when they play, I worry every day.
What's a mother for?

I worry when they're cold,
I worry when they're hot.
I worry when they're sick,
now what else have I forgot?

I worry when they're sad.
I worry when they're mad.
I worry when they hit,
I worry they'll get bit.
What's a mother for?

I worry when it rains.
I worry when it snows.
I worry when there's ice,
and when the wind blows.

I worry in the summer that they'll drown in the pool.
I worry in the fall about their transition to school.
I worry in the winter that they'll get a bad chill.
I worry in the spring that they'll tumble down a hill.
What's a mother for?

I worry when it thunders,
I worry when there's lightning.
I worry at nature's wonders.
It's really rather frightening.

I worry about the present.
I worry about the past.
I worry about the future,
and will this really last?

I worry for my children
who are just too young to know
about all the things there are
that make me worry so.

I learned it from *my* mother
who worries about me
and about all her grandchildren
and great-grandchildren-to-be.

A mother's job is never done.
We worry night and day.
It's really rather worrisome,
but that's why I always say...

"That's what a mother is for!"

O

# Breakfast at Grandma's

Breakfast at Grandma's is a special time of day.
Sharing toast and French coffee is my favorite way
To bask in the quiet of the early morning hour
Before going upstairs and taking a warm shower.

I watch Grandma's cheeks slowly turn pink
As she prepares our coffee just near the sink.
She huffs and puffs mustering all of her might
To carry out this ritual after the night.

The smell of coffee filters through the air
Making our senses fully aware
That soon we'll be savoring this liquid treat
That is better than anything we could eat.

Breakfast with Grandma is a precious time.
I love to be with this Grandma of mine.
There's no one quite like her, of that I'm sure.
She has a warm and special allure.

She's short and plump with silky white hair.
Her skin is soft and colored fair.
She lives in a house that's grand and old,
Where many a historic tale she has told.

Pictures of our family cover the walls,
And antique carpets line the halls.
Plants and flowers in pots stand still
On tables and on many a window sill.

Cupboards and closets are filled to the brim
With old clothes and yarns, jars and tins,
And mysterious objects that we can only guess
Lie hidden like wonders in a treasure chest.

For grandchildren like me it's an adventure
To see what I can find whenever I venture
Through the cluttered rooms of my grandmother's home.
It's a world of discovery I love to roam.

Grandma is a wonderful part of my past.
The days of childhood have gone by fast.
Yet here we both sit across her table,
Remembering the days when Grandma was still able

To walk without a cane by her side
Which she must use like a trusted guide.
We sit and share the simple pleasure
Of coffee in the morning — there's nothing better.

Grandma is often tired now.
Life seems overwhelming somehow.
But her face alights, and she perks herself up
When she pours French coffee into her cup.

It's simple treats that make her feel glad,
When the aches and pains of life feel bad.
And spending time together is special for me.
It's the way grandparents and grandchildren should be.

Years from now I'll look back in time
At the moments I've shared with this Grandma of mine.
No morning coffee will ever compare
To the steaming cups that my grandmother shared.

○

# September Sounds

The alarm clock rings,
and school bells sing.
Voices groan from under covers.
It is time to rise from summer's slumber.

September sounds, once distant,
are now so near.
It is the start of another school year.

Buses roar down the road,
off to pick up their precious load.
At every house, doors slam shut
as kids rush out to meet the bus.

The school building, once silent,
now resounds with great shouts,
laughing and crying,
children running about.

New shoes clacking on polished floors
protected from stains of the great outdoors.
Chalk pecking against smooth blackboards,
children's whispers, then order restored.

Houses are silent until 3 o'clock
when buses screech onto the block.
Delivering children back to their homes
where they are free to play and roam.

Book bags banging on kitchen counters
bulging with school papers, torn and tattered.
Kids munching on afternoon snacks,
then running outdoors to play out back.

The afternoons are getting short

with little time for kids to sport.
The season of homework has begun,
an end to leisure and summer fun.

The sounds of summer begin to fade,
the splashing of pools, where kids used to wade.
Bouncing of balls on the pavement outside,
the whizzing of bikes as children ride by.

The sounds of autumn seem fresh and clear,
heralding the start of a new year.
Summer's song is a long-distant friend,
that fills our memories 'til school year's end.

Listen closely and you will hear
the music of fall, the tunes so dear.
Listen to the September sounds
as they wondrously and joyously resound.

# The Last Child

You are my baby, you are my last.
My child-bearing days are past.
It makes me sad that I'll have no more,
and yet our future holds so much in store.

As we watch you grow from baby to child,
our lifestyle becomes a little more wild.
We say "goodbye" to diapers and wipes,
pacifiers, bottles, and sleepless nights.
And say "hello" to the toddler years,
full of potties, tantrums, falls, and tears.

Seeing you run and watching you climb,
scraping your knees and playing in grime.
You are full of wonder, excitement and glee,
unafraid of new heights — that scares me!

You try to keep pace with your sister and brother,
while ignoring the pleas of your cautious mother.
You want to do all the things they do,
even though you haven't even reached age two!

I know I'm too nervous as I see you climb stairs,
tripping on shoelaces, those close calls are a scare!
And yet you refuse to take hold of my hand,
you want your independence, to take your own stand.

And just when I think that you need me no more,
you call out my name with a look I adore.
Full of tender love and quiet devotion,
you come to restore that bond that's unspoken.

Your small hands reach out to hold me tight.
You little legs cling to me with all their might.
Your warm body and mine come together as one,
like the day you were born, my precious young son.

I treasure such moments, they will not last.
You're growing up now, much too fast.
And on nights when I rock you to sleep,
feeling your soft breath against my cheek,
I smell the sweetness of your baby scent,
and know that you are heaven sent.

I know that I'm sentimental;
being a mother, it's elemental.
But since you are the last baby of mine,
I am compelled to remember these special times.

When you're older and are gone from our home
I'll read this poem and ponder how you've grown.
I'll close my eyes and remember this night,
when I wrote these words, and how they felt so right.

◯

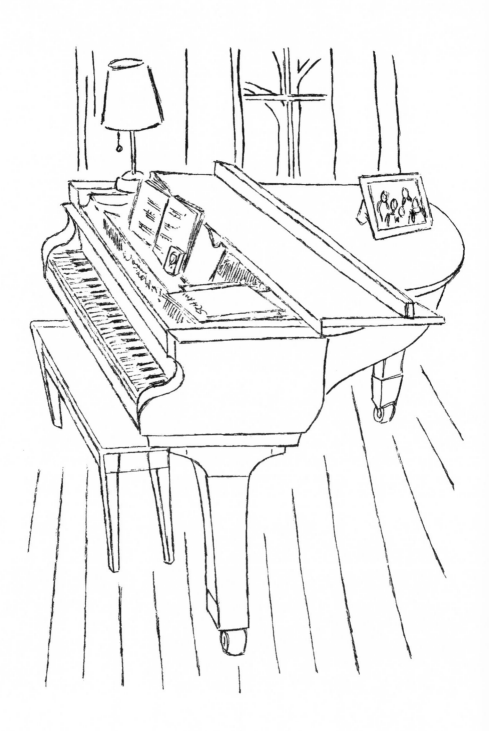

# The Piano

The piano has been in our family for as long as I can remember. It has always sat prominently in the sunny living room of our home, its grand keys gleaming and beckoning us to play.

Small hands learned first notes. My sister and I used Leila Fletcher's first piano books and a dozen-a-day exercises to learn about lines and spaces, the names of musical notes, and the positioning of hands. Intervals and chords became part of our vocabulary. We mastered simple, then increasingly complex, musical pieces during our childhood. Basic compositions were followed by concertos, nocturnes, and preludes. As we matured, we added the music of Beethoven, Mancini and Chopin to our repertoire. The ticking of the metronome helped us to keep time — as time ticked on in our lives. We played waltzes, polonaises, and sonatas. We learned to cooperate with each other by playing duets together. My parents opened their home to other music students over the years as they hosted piano recitals from time to time. We became adept at performing for others and began to appreciate the talent of other musicians. We also learned a bit about poise in the process!

My mother marked the occasion of her 40th birthday by beginning her own study of this magnificent instrument. Learning comes more slowly when you're older, but she pursued her music with a 40-year-old passion. The piano challenged her, but she tackled it with mature determination. She taught us by example that perseverance can help you overcome difficult obstacles.

The piano helped us develop our musical sensibilities. It instilled in us values of hard work and discipline. It added beauty, melody and harmony to our lives. We came to appreciate the complexity of seemingly simple, fine sounds and to realize that each note is an integral part of a greater musical body.

The piano has stood mostly silent over the years since we grew up and left home, but its majestic presence has continued to grace the living room in my parents' house. On top of it have been placed framed photographs —

pictures of grown children, and a new generation of grandchildren. Their faces smile eagerly from the piano. New little hands now wait, ready to tackle those gleaming black and white keys.

The decision to pass on this piano to the next generation has been a difficult one for my parents. It is more than just a physical move — out of one home and into another. It is an acknowledgement that our lives are moving forward. The clock ticks on, moving constantly like the metronome that once helped us control the beat of our music.

We cannot slow down the passage of time, yet we can savor our memories while fulfilling our dreams for tomorrow. Now in my 40th year, I will sit once again at this piano that has played such a significant role in my life. As my children now prepare for their upcoming piano lessons, I look forward to listening to simple notes that will fill our home with musical possibilities.

The piano is a symbol of my parents' love, and of the passion we share for music. I will think of my mother and father each time I sit at the piano in my own living room. We have been given a family treasure, a musical heirloom. We will cherish this piano and will welcome it into our home like a member of the family.

O

# We Were Once a Couple... Now a Family

You are my husband, you're my best friend.
My devotion and love for you has no end.
You've heightened the joy that's in my life.
I am so blessed that we're husband and wife.

I remember the day we stood at the altar
We were resolute. We did not falter.
Our love for each other has continued to grow.
Along with our children, all three in a row.

We've established our roles as father and mother,
And taken a break from romancing each other.
Parenthood is a partnership made for two,
That leaves little time for just me and you.

It's a challenging job that changes each day.
We tackle it together, come what may.
From tears of joy at the birth of each child,
To keeping ourselves calm when kids get too wild.

We've supported each other on sleepless nights,
And calmed each other through kids' noisy fights.
Our children test our patience and skill,
With their tenacity and increasing strong will.

Our shared sense of humor helps keep us sane.
We have to rely on it time and again.
Life with young children brings great delight,
But also leaves us running day and night.

We try to stay calm and to do the right thing,
But we can't guarantee the success that will bring.
We help each other keep an even perspective
When one of us sometimes feels less than objective!

We balance each other as a couple should,
And try to elicit in each other what's good.
We're committed to our kids and our life together.
As parents, it's a rewarding but trying endeavor.

We were once a couple, now we're parents of three.
We've learned to adapt very happily.
While we try to maintain a sense of romance,
Once our children are grown, we'll have more of a chance.

For now we settle for an occasional date,
But our love for each other remains first-rate.
I know that our future holds much more in store.
I cherish you now and will forevermore.

O

*A poem for my mother, Pearl Simmons*

*by Noah Simmons, age 13*

# A Mom is Something Other

A mother is a mother
But a mom is something other
A mom is always there for you
This last line is very, very true
A mom will always stand up for her child
Even if he has been very wild
Most of us don't know what we got
We take our moms for granted and then by the draw of the lot

They're gone and now they won't come back
And we finally realize how much they kept us on track
How much they meant to us
Always seeing us off, making sure we got safe to the bus
We think back and remember all the good times
But now they're only memories stuck in our minds
We loved our moms
But for some reason
We could never express this to them
When they were alive
But now it's too late and she'll never see us drive
Or grow up and have a wife and children
This poem goes out to everyone who's been in
A tragedy where they lost a loved one
A mother, daughter, or maybe a son
I feel your pain because I loved my mom
And on this very special day
I just wanted to say
That we're thinking of you
And our love has not been drained
And Mother's Day will never be the same
Because we'll always have the pain
In our heart
Because you had to depart
So happy Mother's Day, Mom
We'll love you forever
And we will never
Stop loving you
And maybe it's true
That you're in a better place
Smiling down on us
Through your radiant face

O

*May 11, 2003 — Mother's Day*

# EPILOGUE

Passion. Pearl loved life passionately, and everything she did was marked by the intensity of her feelings. Her relationships with her family and friends were all-important, to which she gave freely of her time and energy. She was passionate about both learning and teaching. She spent countless volunteer hours teaching parents how to have positive relationships with their children, and how to keep them safer and more secure. Writing — articles, letters, and poems — was a calling. Pearl wrote poems for many occasions — birthdays, anniversaries, the start of school, births, and deaths — that expressed her joy of living and her deep love for family and friends. Her poems, in turn, gave joy and insight to those who read them.

Elegance. Pearl was a true lady, in every sense of the word — refined, tasteful, cultured. Pearl dressed elegantly and carried herself gracefully; even her smile and laugh were elegant. Whether sipping espresso at a cafe in Paris or getting down and dirty (literally) on an archaeological dig in Israel, Pearl exuded an air of elegance and composure that gave comfort and strength to those around her. Even bumping into things in the dark, she did with distinction. Pearl was a true jewel.

I miss terribly my passionate, elegant Pearl, my wife and best friend. Fortunately, some small part of her lives on through her poetry and in the memories of the countless people whose lives she touched. Through this book, a labor of love by her friends, her memory endures.

— *Reid Simmons, May 2003*

# DONORS

For more than 10 years, Pearl Simmons was a dedicated instructor for the *Positive Parenting Program* of Children's Hospital of Pittsburgh. These courses of three to six sessions are offered at community sites to give parents practical ideas on how to build healthy, happy relationships with their children. Thanks to the generosity of the following donors, all of the proceeds from the sale of this book will support the *Positive Parenting Program* to help perpetuate the parenting philosophy and values that Pearl held so dear.

*The Barkowitz Family*

*Elaine, Gerry, Stacy, Harrison, and Matthew Barron*

*Lainey, Adam, Miles, and Julia Becker*

*Sue and Steve Bertenthal*

*Beth El Congregation of the South Hills*

*Beth El Congregational Religious School*

*Beth El Nursery School*

*Women's Study Group, Beth El Congregation*

*Joseph Bruno*

*Sheila and Alvin Catz*

*Celia Shapiro and Bob Dorfman*

*Marla and Avraham Feather & Family — Jerusalem*

*The Feuer Family*

*Susan and Richard Finder & Family*

*Brenda Gregg*

*Chris and Iris Harlan*

*Thelma and Andrew Herlich*

*Georgia and Bob Hernandez*

*Denise, Bob, Hilary, and Matt Hodes*

*Sidney and Maxine Hoffman*

*Huber Children*

*Paul Impellicceiri and Mollie Neuman*

*Dayna Jornsay-Hester Charles Koven*

*Robert and Karen Krohner & Family*

*The Kushner Family*

*Brenda and Richard Levenson*

*Daniel, Janice, Marissa, and Zachary Levenson*

*Rosanne and Clifford Levine*

*Doretta and Alan Levine, Charlotte and Herbert Mandel*

*The Mantel Family*

*F. Melton Adult Mini-School, South Hills Class of 2001–03*

*The Misrahi Family*

*The Mologne Family — Dave, Margaret, Thomas, Nicholas, and John*

*James A. Morris*

*Janet and Jack Mostow & Family*

*Brad and Bernita Myers*

*Drs. Leigh Nadler and Johanna Drickman*

# DONORS
(continued)

Casey and Marilyn Neuman

Dori and David Oshlag

The Patterson Family

John and Diane Pion
& Family

Geri, Steven, Jacob, Sydney,
and Rayna Recht

Tina and Howard Rieger

Drs. Susan and Eric Safyan

Mindy Sanjana

Naomi Levenson Schaffer,
Jacob, and William Schaffer

Liora and Ed Schlesinger

Cathy and James Schuster

Susan and Larry Schuster

Daniel and Shelly Seigel,
Hannah, Shoshana,
and Shira

Reid, Noah, Rachel, and
Joshua Simmons

Bobbie Simmons

Lorraine and Henry Simmons

Shraga and Keren Simmons
& Family — Israel

Bill and Patty Snyder

South Hills Interfaith
Ministries

Robbin and Paul Steif

Dr. Bertrand and
Shirley Stolzer

Kathleen Stoner

Barbara Strauss

The Tabachnicks

Nathan and Zara Tabor

Dale Teitelbaum

Sol and Lin Toder

Lori-Belle, Dan, Shira, Marisa,
and Ally Underberger

Hugh and Barbara Watters

Nancy Wein and
Daniel Baldwin

Ross and Naomi Wheeler

Dr. and Mrs. Richard Wolf

For more information about the life and work
of Pearl Simmons, please visit the website:

http://www.cs.cmu.edu/~reids/pearl